A SPIRITUAL JOURNEY

A SPIRITUAL JOURNEY

Poems that Talk to Humble Hearts

VOLUME I

Joseph P. Policape

To order additional copies of this book, contact:
Xlibris Corporation
1-888-795-4274
www.Xlibris.com
Orders@Xlibris.com
32220

ACKNOWLEDGEMENTS

Special thanks to Junior DelaCruz my photographer, and to my special colleagues Jocelyn Joseph and Walson Thomas for their encouragement and good advice.

CONTENTS

GOD THE FATHER

I blessed thee! You are God the Father,
You the creator in the beginning you created
the universe, the earth, and the atmosphere.
It was darkness when you started.
You created light in each hemisphere.

Blessed are thou Lord, you are spirit,
I pray Oh Father with your spirit fill
Me and replenish me with thy might
So with thy love, I can obey your will.
Keep me to light daily in thy sight.

Blessed are thou, you are omnipotent
Lord, everything is possible for thee.
You are the only one that is super-eminent
I pray Oh Father; under your dictates keep me,
With thy power, help me to live under thy laws.

Blessed are thou Father, you are omniscient
In your omniscience, you know the number of my hairs.
You watch over the sparrows in the past and the present.
Oh Father God, giver of peace! Listen to my prayers
And give me thy patience to serve you permanently.

Blessed are thou Lord! You are holy and righteous,
Dear Lord, my protector, send the Helper to me,
While in thy dwelling, keep me safe every hour,
so that I can know thy power and personally know thee,
and in thy presence, I'll sing your name in the last hour.

Blessed be God. He is a loving and good god,
Blessed thee, thank thee for giving us your only Son.
Oh, Father, protect your children with your mighty rod.
I give thanks to thee Lord, your word is good.
Blessed are thou Lord, thank you for being our god.

JESUS THE SON

Oh, Alleluia! Alleluia! Emmanuel is given!
Oh, blessed his only begotten son, how marvelous unto us!
He has the most honorable name and for us he bled,
He has been called Wonderful Counselor, Mighty God and glorious.
We now can bow down to confess for wrong things we said.

You are the Son who came to save us, existed in the beginning.
You are the logos, the bread of life and the word of the Father.
You are our light and through thee we are comforted.
You are the way, grace and truth and in you I'd rather
Put all my confidences, beliefs and in you I'd rather trust.

The Lord feed his people. He calls upon every man now
to honor the Son, honor the holy spirit as we adore the Father.
Jesus the savior of all people let all creatures worship thee.
And through thee, let every tongue proclaim God as the Father
Before you, Jesus our Lord, every knee should bow.

Thank you Lord for your greatness. You vowed to remit our sin.
He avowed to the disciples that the Father and he are one.
He assures rest, joy, love and peace. He is sovereign.
And he pledges to be with us and never leave us alone.
I will wait to get into his kingdom to play a tambourine.

Let us all extol the domination of our Lord Jesus Christ.
Jesus shall reign! I can't wait for the sign of the Son of Man.
The saints shall be happy in heaven and with Jesus they will not be enticed.
We shall praise him as King of kings, not just as the son of man.
His right hand shall be filled with justice and he shall carry my merit as a sinner.

Shout joyfully to our King! He is the Prince of Peace for eternity
He reigns forever and in his government, there shall be no war.
Exult the Lord Oh Nations! There will be true verdict and equity.
O, Yes! Jesus shall lock Satan, and he shall never reopen the door.
Jesus our Lord will be labeled everlasting King for all eternity.

THE HOLY SPIRIT

You are the Spirit of truth, my counselor, I heard about thee
moving in the engulfed darkness since the beginning.
You are the power of the Father, and you my eyes shall see.
You have controlled all creation since the beginning.
You were witnessing the universe created and the sea.

I praise you Oh Holy Spirit! You are the spirits of glory and truth.
You watch over me day and night. What a divine mission!
Like Boaz in the field. We surrender to you like Ruth.
We ponder your loving kindness for you love as the Son.
We praise you for you have protected King David in his youth.
You protected me and you sanctified me under the sun.

Oh Holy Spirit! You, the Son, and the Father are a blend.
You are the water of life. You have existed since the creation.
Alleluia! Alleluia! You shall be with us till the end.
You have protected me just as the Father and the Son.
Alleluia! Alleluia! In thee I find my protection
Through you Oh Holy Spirit! I have an omnipotent friend.

Glory be to God, He sent you to speak of Jesus as King of kings.
You are the one who reveals God the Father to us.
You are powerful and capable of knowing all things.
You are good to me. You make me feel blessed.
You have kept your children hidden under your wings.
Oh true counselor, I hear you speak in my ear when I sin.

Not with thee Oh Holy Spirit, where can I find wisdom?
Not with thee Oh Holy Spirit, how can I be pious and cheer?
Alleluia! I am free for you are the spirit of faith and freedom.
Alleluia! I have not fear for you are the commander of the sphere.
You are holy, Oh, counselor! You are the spirit of God.
How can I live without you? You are our water, oil, wind, and fire.

Oh counselor! You had been sent by Almighty to chide me.
Oh Holy Spirit! You are the third person of the Trinity.
Oh Holy Spirit! You are the Spirit of Christ, so I bow to thee.
You are my joy, my peace and you are our god of Divinity.
You are a true protector. You protect the water and sea.
Thank you, Oh, Holy Spirit. You are always with me.

ADAM AND EVE

You were repudiated from the Garden of Eden
For selling your birthright! What's virtuous in thee?
You had been kicked out from the garden.
You had eaten from the forbidden tree.
For you only toil for your own craving even in Eden.
And go against your own creator who created thee.

The cunning animal seduced her.
Oh, Adam should have left the woman alone in the garden.
She lost her virginity and saw everything blur.
The snake laughed at Adam and Eve in Eden.
Yeah! They ate the sweet poison fruit and deserved to die.

Dust, isn't it what you are made of?
God put his goodness in you, and now your soul is poisoned.
Death descended into your life just like a curse from above.
Ah! You are a foolish one, full of evil passion too.
You've depraved yourself and have destroyed the good in you.

Why did you disobey the Father who wanted you to be saved?
Why did you allow Satan to take you back to the dust?
You have many grievances that made you misbehave.
How would you abide with God now who is just?
After he molded you in his hands, and you were saved.
Uh! Your heart was never with your creator, and your action is disgusting.

You ate the poison fruit and then began to shout.
You made a fool of yourself in Eden.
And from the garden you were thrown out.
Oh, Adam, why did you eat the forbidden fruit in the garden?
Ah! Now you inherited the serpent's pride.
God got angry and shouted, "Out, out from my garden!"
Adam, you should have been on God's side!

You exposed yourself in God's presence.
You acquired from the serpent division.
Don't you know God is omnipresent?
And he created you with heavenly notion in you?
Adam! How you accepted to lose God's provision?
Oh, Adam! Your creator couldn't admit you.

Adam! God judged you according to your heart
The snake's expertise in lying, couldn't you see?
For seducing you, he shall climb on his belly forever.
And eat dust forevermore, walk on his belly and the
Serpent's offspring and that of Eve will be enemies forever.
Ah . . . you shall never abide in the kingdom of God till the end.

GOD'S LAWS

Who can change that?
God's laws are firm and sweet.
Who can change that?
God's laws are firm and sweet.
Who can ask God to change his mind?

God said to Eve,
"Woman, you're the subject of Adam
and will always push children in pain."
Who can change that?
God's laws are firm and sweet.
Who can ask God to change his mind?

God said to Adam,
"Why listen to thy wife and sin, Oh man?
You must work hard on the terrain
to feed yourself, wife, and children, and
You're all subject to eternal death and pain.

God said to the serpent,
"Serpent, you caused my children to sin,
You shall forever walk on your belly.
And the Son of Man shall bruise your head."
Who can change that?
God's laws are firm and sweet.
Who can ask God to change his mind?

THE GUARDIAN ANGELS

How wonderful are those celestial
Beings. I can't wait to sing with the angels.
They are beautiful, terrestrial.
Oh, I can't wait to see the archangels.
But the angels are beautiful, extraterrestrial.
In my dream I saw the angels in the mist of the skies.
They go down and rise, down and rise.

The angels are the strongest invisible
Army on the earth and the heavens,
And they are also visible.
In my dream I saw up to seven
Angels in the mist of the skies,
They go down and rise, down and rise
Between the seas and cosmos, Oh, how wise!

I saw them sitting on the wings of the winds.
They carried the tornadoes in their palms.
But I don't know what's in their minds.
The tornadoes are like bombs.
They have the whole world in their hands.
To any other army they are incomparable.
And next to them I see God stands.

Did you know they are always available?
I saw them piloting armed airplanes.
To any other army they are incomparable.
And I saw God among them making plans
On how they are going to save humanity.
On the day of rapture, we will be in their hands.
My angel will save me; my angel has a good personality.

Oh, how wonderful are the feet of the angels.
They saved Lot and his family at Sodom.
Oh, how mighty are the works of the guardian angels.
They visited Manoah at the birth of Samson.
A visit by the angels is by God's grace.
Would you like to be visited by angels?
When you see an angel, you see God face to face.

The angels praised and shook
God's throne and they sang.
Trust me; you will love how the angels look.
You will love seeing them speak in tongues.
The angels will add your name in their book
Till Satan will be under you feet forever.

SIN

You brought God's wrath to the world entirely.
You made God remember not the offenses of man.
You entered Cain; he killed Abel, and that was deadly.
You are anathema, Oh, sin; I'm not your clan.
You are a debilitate god with the wrong plan.

As the son of man, I walk on your head,
I won the battle when Jesus came into my life.
And forever you have been fled.
Sin, depart thou from me; you are not my wife.
The unblemished Lamb of God is here.
You're squalid, viperous, and rife
Satan's deeds are manifested in you.

You're born for divestiture.
You have been cast off from Elysium,
You are an abomination that brings woe to us to endure.
You are my enemy. You are not my chum.
You are a tragedy and dumb.
I cast thee in the abyss for eternity.

ON THE LORD'S DAY

The lofty will cry on the Lord's Day.
Before Jesus, they will be shy.
For God calls on every man today,
"Stop living in such a world of lies."

Man must leave evil; come to God's side.
Oh God! Open his eyes let him see I pray!
He must accept Jesus as Savior and he won't cry.
One must open his eyes of faith to find the way.

Soon and very soon Satan will be bound.
Help me think of this beautiful day, Lord!
Did you see Saddam come out of the ground?
Every name will appear on God's switchboard.

Man must find Jesus a place in him to hide.
Saddam went into a hole but was found
If Bin Laden comes out, he will be fried.
O! when I think of Jesus' Day, this is profound!

If there's no place to hide from America
Can you hide from Christ at the sound
of the trumpet? You will be found even in Africa.
All breakers of God's laws will be bound.

WHERE ARE YOU GOING TO HIDE?

Jesus knows who you are, and he will find you.
Every day you beat him when you mistreat the poor.
Every time you mistreat a brother, you nail him for
Either you have abused the women and the poor,
God never closes his eyes. He saw you for sure.
He is in control. He knows your past and future.

The day shall come when the sun won't shine.
The day shall come when the stars will be falling.
Regimes of the earth will see the sign
And will be put to shame when Jesus is calling
For every believer to come and dine,
Make a reservation now before the roads are crawling.

The day shall come when the moon will turn into blood.
The day shall come when God's people will assemble.
The day shall come when the earth will turn into flood.
And God knows who you are, and you will tremble.
Jesus saw when you threw your broth in the mud.
Now he is coming, where will you hide on the Lord's Day?

MY JESUS

Jesus, add my name to your team.
You are the chief above every boss.
I want to be part of you regime.
I pray, Oh, Lord, keep me near the Cross.
Where there is a precious fountain
Facilitate me to fix my eyes on Calvary
I want to meet Jesus on God's mountain.
There, I will be freed from Satan, my enemy.

I love you my Jesus, Savior and King,
I feel your mighty hand of love
In the summer as well as in the spring
You are holding me from heaven above.
Oh, I feel safe in the mighty hand of Christ,
Oh, hold me with the power of your love.
Hold me nearer to the cross where there is light.
I want to meet Jesus on God's mountain.
Where there is a precious fountain.

Oh my Jesus, add my name to your team
of heavenly citizens Oh my savior supreme.
In heaven, there is joy and a healing stream.
Jesus, my Lord, you are the chief above every boss.
I wait for thee to take me to the paradise of my dream.
Jesus my savior and Lord, help me stay near the cross
So someday I can meet you, my savior, on your mountain
Where there is pure water of life in your precious fountain.

ONE DAY LIKE TODAY

One day like today, we'll be done,
The faithful will enter their dwelling,
In that city Jesus will be the sun.
In the river of life we'll be swimming.
When Jesus comes on that day, it will be fun.
Our pains and diseases will be gone
And in Jesus's kingdom we'll rest.
Oh, in heaven where it will be fun.
Yeah! I will rest near Jesus' breast.

Oh! God will open the city gates,
Rightful Christians will enter
We'll see Jesus' dazzling face in God's states.
On that day, Jesus will be our mentor.
We'll see the beloved, who preceded us,
In heaven with Jesus I will be singing.
My labors and trials will end,
Glory, Alleluia! Forever with Jesus I'll rest,
Oh, I will rest nearer to Jesus' breast.

Those who die will rise again,
Their corpses will come back to life.
We all, Christians, will rise without stain.
We will leave the world of strife.
We'll live in heaven without pain.
Oh, we will see Jesus' dazzling face.
We'll have entitlement to the tree of life.
Glory to God! We'll rest at Jesus' place
Rest in heaven where there is eternal life.

AWAKE, OH, MY SOUL

Awake! Awake, Oh, my soul.
The haze of sin put you to sleep.
I pray, Oh, Jehovah, take control.
You are my God. I am your sheep.
Fill me Oh Holy Spirit; give me self-control,
My soul can awake from sleep,
And I can hear your voice when you call.

I pray, come to breathe in me.
The haze of sin put me to sleep.
Oh, Lord, remember me; I am a refugee.
Sanctify me, your face I ought to see.
Oh, Holy Spirit, come in my heart, sweep,
And with your spirit fill me like a fruitful tree.

The time is at hand for me to reap.
Oh, Lord of peace, sanctify me
Wholly, body, soul, and spirit,
so that I can be worthy in your sight.
Lord, help me to stay blameless like a sheep
So I can always be ready even if you come tonight.

REJOICE

Oh, my soul, rejoice! Rejoice!
The nations of the earth are clever,
But they don't know how to make good choices.
Or they would choose Jesus to bring peace in Jerusalem.
Jesus says with his own voice,
He will establish peace in Zion and Bethlehem.

The nations will lose their pride
When my Savior, Jesus will appear,
O, My Lord! I see leaders run and hide.
Jesus will say a word, nations will disappear
Government will be plunged, establishment **quieted**.
And Jesus will reign forever, and Satan is discredited.

Oh, my soul, rejoice! Rejoice.
Oh, my soul, rejoice and bless the Lord!
The poor will be fed when they hear Jesus' voice.
The rich will be cold when they hear their rewards.
Every creature will hear Jesus' voice without a choice.
Jesus will reign and abiding to earth after all.
As King of kings, he will be seen by every eye.

Oh, my soul, rejoice for God won't cease
Until the people of Israel live in peace.
And the surrounding nations will try to hide in the sea.
This is not daydreaming, Jesus'eye we shall see.
Jesus will reign and he will be the only guide.

ENTERING GOD'S PRESENCE

You're entering the presence of the Lord
Be silent, be silent, be silent.
Jesus is King upon his throne,
Be silent, be silent, be silent.
Shout with the same accord
Then be silent; be silent, before the Lord.

You're entering the gate of the Lord
Be silent, be silent, be silent.
Be ready to receive your reward.
Forever and ever, forever and ever,
Amen! Alleluia, for the Lord is here
Jesus is the King for all men who are sincere.

You're entering the presence of the Lord,
Be silent, be silent, be silent
Can you hear the seraphim singing in the same accord!
Bow before the Lord and be confident.
Listen to the seraphim saying, "There is peace."
There is peace in God for those who repent,
And Jesus is king; our troubles will ease.

COME NOW, MY DEAR JESUS

Oh, if you hear the voice of the Lord today.
Come! Bow down before him without delay.
The Lord will make his salvation known
When on this earth there shall be no cyclone.
All the end of the earth will see his face.
All our sins through his blood shall erase.
His right hand will win our victory.
The world shall terminate, but with the Lord I will be.

I know the world is terminating,
But my heart is not beating.
My King Jesus is coming.
Oh, I am thirsty for the meeting.
Jesus alone will save me from perishing.
In this world of iniquity and saddening
Oh, come now, Jesus, my King.
Come now, my dear Jesus, the world is fleeting.

I will bless the lord on the day he comes.
My soul shall be glory in his bosoms.
My departure to heaven is now at hand.
I am not belonging here, heaven is my homeland.
I have been on this earth serving God willingly.
In the hand of his enemy I have suffered badly.
But I fear no evil for I know the world is terminating.
I will see Jesus face to face. I am thirsty for the meeting.

IF I MUST GO

If today my life is over on this earth.
If tomorrow I am getting older,
If it happened I must travel, and I know
Jesus will carry me on his shoulder.
And I know where I will be after leaving this earth.

I will be in the bosom of Christ.
I will sing for Jesus the great scientist.
I will extol him and dance with him.
I will bless him and play with him.
I will sit with Jesus beyond,
And drink water from his pond.

Oh! In heaven I will swim,
Heaven is so magnificent.
I will sing for Jesus and dance with him
Oh Alleluia! My god is magnificent.
I will laugh with Jesus beyond,
And drink water from his pond.

If today my life is over on this earth
My body decides to go to sleep,
If it happened I must travel.
My time is closer, but I know where I will be.
My gracious Lord! I am getting older
But in heaven everything will be all right.
For Jesus will carry me on his shoulder.

ALLELUIA FOREVERMORE

Some day my life will be over,
In this world of trouble I won't stay.
In heaven I will stand like a soldier.
While on earth my body will decay,
In heaven I will sing and pray,
"Alleluia for the Cross."

I will praise the Lord as I enter his gate.
I will sing his glory with joy in my heart.
Jesus will welcome me for my fate.
I will bless Jesus and he will call me a part,
To forgive me, my sin will dissipate.
I will bow before him with all my heart.
And I will praise the Lord forevermore.

I will dance like an angel,
I will sing Alleluia for the cross.
I will sing in God's chapel.
Oh yes, I will sing Alleluia for the cross.
I will serve my god forevermore.
And with Jesus I will fear nevermore.

I AM EMPLOYED

I am a servant working for Jesus, my King,
He is the greatest boss that ever lived.
I do not have the riches of the world, but for Jesus I sing.
Oh, Alleluia! With Jesus, I will survive.
Alleluia! Praise Jesus my redeemer. I will survive
Glory to God my King! I will survive
I will survive for Jesus gives me a song to sing.

Since he hired me, I've found peace that Jesus gives
Oh, I've found joy that the world could not give me.
I have a house in the sky where Jesus and I will live.
Jesus work is holy. As his employee I will forever be free.
Amen, amen, alleluia with Jesus I will live.

Jesus our King is the only one with the heavenly key.
Work for Jesus the mighty King who is always faithful.
Let those who are suffering come on your knees,
Tell Jesus your plea. Every other boss is brutal.
Then he will save you and give you a song to sing.

DEAR LORD, COME DOWN TODAY

Dear Lord, hear my voice crying.
"Holy Spirit, I cry, come down today."
Lord, you see the poor are dying
I cry, "Oh, Lord, come down today
Oh, Holy Spirit, you are our counselor today."
I cry, "Save your children from dying."

Holy Spirit, come down today.
My heart is bleeding, and my eyes are crying.
Oh, Jesus, mighty king, help me walk from day to day
I tremble when I see my brothers dying
Lord, I tremble when I see people are lying
I cry, "Oh, Lord, come down today."

I cry when I see the children on drugs.
I cry when I hear men are not afraid to kill.
Oh, Lord, families are crying each time a child mugs.
Men dropping bombs on each other still
I cry, dear Lord, "Come down if you will."

THE TRUTH

You should always tell the truth.
Let no one seduce you, try, and try.
When you tell the truth, it hurts the rich.
They turn against you and will send spy
To kill you, put you in jail, but be frank.
Tell the truth even if it hurts the politicians.
Tell the truth; don't be afraid of a war tank.

It hurts the Mafia and the criminal elements.
Even in time of Jesus, it had been that way.
But Jesus was never afraid of the mafia agents.
They killed Jesus who stood in their way.
God is with you; don't be afraid of an imperialist.

They killed John the Baptist before God's eyes.
They killed John F. Kennedy, and now he dies.
They killed Gandhi, a man who was wise.
They killed Martin Luther King Jr. and other good guys.
Don't worry if they kill you, tell the truth.

Remember, as Jesus died, we are all born to die.
Remember how Ahab and Jezebel killed Naboth.
They used their might and thought God did not see them.
The prophet told them the truth, and he wasn't shy.
I will tell the evil men the truth and die just as I am.
God is merciful. It is better to be just in his eye.

AN INVITATION

I don't care who you are, I have been ordained
To tell you about my Jesus, don't ask me,
"What has your religion done for you?" Or
if your religion is good, but to know Jesus is the key,
to know Jesus as your King. You should strive
To get into my religion, yes, you should strive.
The Lord who is faithful called me to ask you to come
Come; bring yourself to God who can lift all who are falling!

I have to go for Jesus; nobody can tie me with rope.
I have to go for Jesus; he is my director and chief.
I have to go for Jesus; he directs my paths and gives me hope.
Come to me, I will tell you how to live without grief.
If you repent, Jesus can wash you with his soap.
Come to me, I will give you advice on how to believe.

You will be safe in bed and in your journey,
And when you're alone you will fear no harm.
You will always be under the defense of a great attorney.
You will not fall into adultery while in Jesus' arm.
You will walk on the ways of Jesus and drugs will stay far from you.
When you meet my Jesus, you will be happy too.

Come my friend, trust in God. Oh you will be glad.
You will not be hurt by the plague of sexual disorder.
If you want to know about my religion, give me your hand.
Come, your life will change, and we will love one another.
Yes, the criminals, the drug addicts, you too can live without grief.
Come my friend, you have no sacrifice to make, just believe.

THE RICH MAN AND A GOD OF PITY

The rich man looks at his lavish condition
He was near to stubble, he laughs, ha-ha, ho-ho,
He was near to be on fire, but he laughs, and laughs.
In his evil heart, he says, "I have so much money."
In his perverse heart he says, "I don't know what to do."
In his confidence, he laughs, ha-ha, ho-ho.
He laughs, laughs, and laughs
He says, as he laughs and laughs,
"I am in a better position even than God."

Then God cuts man's supply of food.
In his omniscient, he laughs, ha-ha, ho-ho,
He laughs, laughs, and laughs.
Why man raises his head so high?
Why does he have so much pride?
He laughs, ha-ha, ho-ho,
He laughs, laughs, and laughs and says,
"What does a man think he is for him to be so rude?"

The rich man raises his voice high,
He sends his army to destroy and kill
He kills whoever stands his way.
He laughs, ha-ha, ho-ho,
He laughs, laughs, and laughs.
He said, "I have so much power,
I can create a 'new world order,'
and I can dominate the sky."

God sits on his throne and roars,
He laughs, ha-ha, ho-ho,
He laughs, laughs, and laughs
God says, "I will have him start a war
He will not be able to stop it.
And he will learn that
I am the only god in the universe
Who can start and stop a war."

The rich man so confident, went to war,
In spite of big weapons, his army fell miserably.
Man remembers God. He looks up to the heavens,
He looks in the sky. He raises his voice high and
He says, "I praise the Lord, God Most High."
As a creature of God, Man can send their corps,
To start war, to kill the innocents, but God is the only one
Who will forever have control to create peace!

WHY I AM SMILING

I am happy and you ask me why I am smiling.
I am smiling, because I am the one who knows
How good it is to be loved by God the everlasting
I was deep in adversity and abiding among the foes.
Jesus pulled me out and took my burden away.
Jesus gave me power over foes since that day.

I am happy and cheerful, it is because
Satan thought he could put me in pain.
I am the one who knows how painful it was.
I had tears in my eyes when I was in chain.
Jesus set me free, and I am born again.

When I am sad I come to you, Oh thank you, Lord,
When I am sad, you're taking away my pain.
I thank you, Lord, for my life you restored.
I feel your presence when you took away my chain.
For what you have done, I want to thank you, Lord.
Thank you Lord, you set me free, and I'm born again.

THE BEAUTIFUL NAME OF JESUS

Jesus, Savior and mighty King,
His name is the only name my heart is longing for.
Come; sing with me the wonderful name of the mighty King.
Jesus, Jesus, forever, Jesus I love him more.

This is the name the seraphim sings.
Come; sing with me. This is the name the angels sing.
Sing with me the name of Jesus.
Lets sing with me the name of the mighty King.

Oh, sing with me, Jesus is coming soon.
Oh, Alleluia! I won't sing any other name,
Come; sing with me, Jesus in the morning and at noon.
Jesus, Jesus is my Savior without blame.

Sing with me, Jesus, Savior and mighty King,
Jesus is the name I am hungry for.
Come; sing with me. Jesus is the name the angels sing.
Jesus, Jesus, forever, Jesus I love him more.

HEAVEN IS SWEET

I was walking on the road.
It was full of dangers and snares.
Off my back, Jesus took my load,
And he dries my tears.
He puts in my mouth an ode.

Heaven above is sweet, sweet.
It's where my soul will abide
Heaven above is sweet, sweet.
It's where I'll live forever and eat
Manna with Jesus, and I will never die
I will walk with Jesus. Oh how sweet!

He told me he loves me.
And he's the father of grace.
I believed in him, and I am free.
He's the father I want to embrace.
He's watching over me on earth.
He ran with me in the race.
And he gave me a new birth.

Heaven above is sweet, sweet.
It's where my soul will abide
Heaven above is sweet, sweet.
It's where I'll live forever and eat
Manna with Jesus, and I will never die
I will walk with Jesus. Oh how sweet!

COME TO ME, SINNERS

Come to me, sinners
Carry the cross on the road I trace.
Leave everything for me, be winners.
Leave everything with no regret.
I'll show you my face.
And I will pay your debt.

Trail your Savior all the time
Trail him without fears or danger.
Trail your Savior all the time
Through the maze of life to eternity and glory,
and in heaven you will not be a stranger,
And the name of Jesus will be your story.

I'm your Savior and master.
Come to me with your worry,
I am your Savior and pastor.
I can save you from sin, hurry!
I'll be your pastor to save you from danger.
Walk with me through eternity and glory,
And in heaven you won't be a stranger.

JUST FOR YOU

For you, my friend, I went on the cross.
I, Jesus, gave my life for you.
I carried and bled on the cross.
I accepted the nails in my hands and feet.
What have you done for me?

What have you done for me?
I am Jesus your Savior and King.
I left my throne in heaven to save you.
They shredded my clothes.
So some day in my glory, you can sing.

I drank vinegar and gave up my pride.
For you, my friend, I accepted the agonies.
For you my friend I died.
Can you leave it all to follow me?
Why can't you leave all for me?

Oh! My Savior and King, I come.
Accept me in your heavenly kingdom
All I have now is for you alone,
Accept me with my plea and shame.
And let my heart praise your name.

AT THE TABLE

At the communion table,
I bow before Christ.
It's where he wants me to be
At the communion table
I'll praise my God who is able
Till the day comes when his face I'll see.

We kneel at the communion table.
This is the body of the Lord.
Let us praise him who is able.
At the table we are waiting for the reward
While we sing the Jesus' story.
Let's do it in his memory.

Oh, Jesus! We remember thee.
Oh, you shed thy blood for us.
Oh! Let us fix our eyes on the Calvary tree.
Let us sit and wait at the communion table, thus
Till the day comes when your face I'll see.

WHEN YOU TRUST IN GOD

You should fear not, not, and not,
When you pass through the flame
You should fear not, not, and not.
The Lord is always there to take your shame
He said fear not, he can undo every plot.

You should fear not in the hard trials,
You should fear not, not, and not
Your God will always help you keep smiles,
In their way through the Red Sea, he said to Israel to fear not.
If he could do it for Moses, he can walk with you many miles.
And he has your name on files.

The Lord walked with Joseph in Egypt, and he feared not
Though he faced trials, he feared not, not, and not.
He said no to Potiphar's wife
He knew the Lord was watching, he could not
Put his faith in danger, even in strife.

Moses said to the king of Egypt some time ago
"The Lord said, 'Let my people go!'"
He feared not, not, and not.
He feared not and not. Moses stood before the king
in the name of the Lord to let him go,
He feared not, of the serpent's sting.

Gideon destroyed his father's god
He feared not, not, and not.
"If Baal is a god, let him defend himself so."
In the battlefield, the Lord told Gideon who should go.
Fear not in your grief, God understands when you nod.

Like Elijah before Jezebel and Ahab who feared not,
The Lord is with me, why should I fear?
The Lord can stop the dew or the rain if you fear not.
Elijah had done it in the name of his Lord.
We should feared not and not when we trust our God,
We should fear not, not, and not,
God can deliver us out of trouble if we fear not.
If the Lord is with us, what should we fear?

JERUSALEM, HOW LUCKY YOU ARE!

Some time ago, the world was gloom
When a light, splendid, descended
Mary and Joseph did not find a room.
But everyone saw the splendid
star that came to save us from doom.
Oh! Jerusalem, your trouble is ended.
Jesus is here, and you shall not dispel the groom.

Jesus, the Son of God, comes to earth to stay.
Jerusalem, how fortunate you are today!
Jerusalem, call your children to play.
Christ is here; bring your myrrh to pray.
Jerusalem, how fortunate you are today!
God himself visited you on Christmas Day.

Emmanuel is here for every broken heart.
He's here to know your pains.
God loves you so much he sets you apart.
Fear no more; God is here to untie your chains.
Alleluia for Jesus; he comes to reign.
Jesus will reign in every man's heart.
Oh! Jerusalem will sing Alleluia; God reigns.
Jerusalem! Praise the Lord of hosts, for he reigns!
You're no longer the ruined city, you are pretty.

For from you came the King of kings
He is the Lord of lords, who is the God of pity.
Oh! Jerusalem let us hear the angel sing,
Jesus is born; Jerusalem is no longer in chains.

GOD'S HOUSE

This is God's house. In this house we serve the Lord.
The bridegroom is here. This is God's dwelling,
Here is a place where we pray and preach his word.
Alleluia! The Lord is faithful, we go telling,
Others we can only worship him here.
This is not a place where we'll be playing.
We do not slander others in the presence of God we fear.
God's house is not a place for playing.

This is God's house. We must not commit infidelity of any form.
This is God's house. We must be living in sanctification.
Do you know we are a people who should follow God's norms!
Do you know we must be looking for his recognition!
Do you know we can't argue about his commands in any form!
Do you know in his house we can't make false accusation!

Why fighting! This is God's house, and we are not rivals.
Why fighting! We are not serving a god of confusion.
Why lying! We are in search for God's revivals.
Jesus is our orator, don't be in delusion.
The bridegroom is here. This is God's dwelling,
Don't come to tell us about yourself and others,
God is not a god of delusion, go tell
Others Jesus is real and they shall become your brothers.

In this house we speak about the covenant of God.
And that's the only thing that should satisfy us.
In this house we should talk about God and nothing to add.
We are dressed already with his armors, and thus
This is not a place where we can get mad
And we can't neglect his word if we want to be blessed.

This is God's house and from his laws we should not be deviating.
Here we praise God. Our resolution is to go to heaven.
You here to worship and this is your reason to be in this dwelling,
You must be part of the meditating like the eleven
Tell me, why so many hypocrites, so much backbiting in God's dwelling!

IF YOU HAD KNOWN GOD

You'd have been happy and free just like me.
You'd have drunk water from the pond of God,
God's kingdom you'd have been expected to see.
And you'd never have been feeling odd.
You'd have drunk the water of life.
And spiritually, you'd have grown.
God would have granted you peace over strife.
You'd have hope when you're feeling down.

You'd have inherited the Lord's kingdom
You'd have cared not of crying.
You'd not have been afraid of the days of martyrdom.
On the day of Jesus return, you'd be flying.
You'd have known that God can comfort you,
As a servant of God, you'd have been humbled.
And with God everything would have become new.
And trust in God to help you not to stumble.

You'd have known God's promises are near.
And you'd have received God's instructions.
You'd not have been afraid if your way is sheer.
And you wouldn't have been afraid of his destruction.
You'd have worked for peace around you.
And you'd have been called a God's child.
You'd have had worn truthfulness as a shoe.
And you'd have had an infinite smile.

You'd have been buoyant just like trees planted by the river.
You'd have had carried good fruits.
You'd have known that God is coming to deliver
those who have worn the Holy Spirit as boots.
You'd have feared the Lord and he'd have made your route.
You'd taste his goodness and he'd have given you a pure heart.
You'd have made others happy around you.
For Jesus would have set you apart.

Forgiveness and understanding would have been in your heart.
Believe me, there's nothing better in life than knowing God.
You'd have always felt like you had a chart.
And that he has been leading you with his rod.
A man of God has the hope of judging the sinners.
He has the hope of standing with God, watching the evils doomed.
And God would reveal to him and he'd be one of God's winners,
And in the last days, he'll be sitting with God in the same room.

A DAY OF JOY

On Christmas Day, the shepherds heard,
The sound went *zoom,* zoom and *zoom*!
It sounded as the angel of the Lord appeared.
The shepherd beat their drums, *zoom* and *zoom*!
As the angels praised the almighty God on that Day.
Let the world hear the earth will no longer gloom
For God the son comes to take our sins away.
The people of Israel listened and heard the boom.
The angels sing, "Jesus is born in Bethlehem today."

The angels sings, to all people I bring good news.
Christ is born in Bethlehem today, did you hear the boom!
Jesus Christ brings good news for the Gentiles and the Jews
Everyone calls your friends and family, make room,
Good news to those on earth who are feeble.
Jesus is here; the world is no longer doom.
Jesus is born in Bethlehem, the angels say
In Bethlehem Jesus could not find room,
But indeed the promised child is born.

Oh, walk in the light of Christ; it is great joy to all nations
The angel says, "I bring good news for you,
Good news for the Gentile populations,
Good news for the Gentiles and the Jews:
Jesus is born in Bethlehem today."
Can you make room for him in your heart!
Call your friends and family to say, "Hey!"
Christ is here to take away our sins, the explorers see the star.
They came from the east to give the news,
Christ Jesus, the son of God is born today.
They asked, "Where is the baby to be King of the Jews?"

Jesus, the only light for the Gentiles and the Jews,
God son comes to reign; he is born in Bethlehem today.
Jesus is here to save us from fear and bruise.
The children of Israel can now play.
Bethlehem, land of Judah, will no longer sing blues.
But the King of Israel is born on Christmas Day.
The least town of Judea is happy but not from booze,
But the good news is that God is here among men to stay.

GOD IS ALWAYS NEAR

One day I was sick, but I awoke in awe.
I had no money to see a doctor, and I was so ill.
Life became senseless, and death was due.
I listened to a message from God who is always near.
I began to walk in the light of Christ, I was very thrilled
He sent the Holy Spirit in my life; my God is so dear.

Call on Jesus, the King, when you're in awe,
Call on Jesus, the Savior, Jesus is always near.
When you feel hopeless call upon your dear
God; you will find that he is always near.
When every door closes for you, don't feel in awe,
But remember Jesus Christ, the son of God is always near.

Oh, call on Jesus to let the light of his truth shine on you.
Jesus the son of God, the light of the world is always near.
Call on Jesus to bring him peace as a gift to abide in you.
When every door closes for you, Jesus is always near.
Jesus will keep you safe under his bosom, he loves you.
Call on Jesus, he will answer your prayer, he is always near.

GOD FIGHTS FOR THE POOR

I look around the world, only Jesus fights for the poor.
I see most women; they are the mothers of mankind,
They have been abused and disrespected by men.
Men harm their children; and to the women, men are unkind.
They have been treated as if they were never part of creation.
Women are always crying and bleeding inside.
Oh, God Almighty! I pray for their liberation!

I look around the world, I see some poor men,
They are fathers like any other men; they have not been respected.
To those poor men, other men feel they are superior,
And for that reason they have been maltreated.
They have been put to jail and accused of things unknown to them.
Those in power have done all these things to make a poor man feel inferior.
Oh, God Almighty! It is shameful what a poor man has to suffer!

God you know how, I disdained people who feel that they are superior.
God our father, I prefer to die than being treated inferior.
I prefer to sleep outside than living inside with a man that mistreats the poor.
A poor man, who stands up for his right, God sees him as a warrior,
A man that abuses the poor, God considers him as a conspirator.

I see some men who are disrespecting the poor to show their grandeur.
I also see those same men gravitate down to the ground like dust
Carried by the winds, and I see a man; he uses his authority to steal from the poor,
He dies poorer than the poor does, and before his death, I see him lament.
It is the same for the aristocrats who use God's holy name in vain.

Before God's kingdom, I see those who steal from the poor are in mourning.
It is Judgment Day; before the throne, they are being called lawbreakers.
Because they make the poor and our women suffer by their prejudice.
They cause pain but feel fine because they are moneymakers.
Ah, they are so evil, they make anyone different from them suffer.
In their funerals, they take their bodies to church, to pray for paradise.
I see God throw them out from his throne and say to them,
"Get out, murderers and sorcerers, no place for evildoers in my kingdom!"

GOD ISN'T ABSENT IN EVERYTHING

After a last rite ended, it was cold when I came out from the cathedral.
I saw by the chapel a poor man, nearly naked, and he was suffering.
I looked at the blind man's situation, and I was angry and enraged.
He was depressed, hurt, crying, and sitting in mud as I was witnessing.
The Cathedral is a splendor; the saints were insensitive to the man's afflictions.
I saw one put a stone in his plate; then I ran to his rescue with tears in my eyes.

The man pushed me away, "I don't need your help," he told me coldly.
"Let them put stones on my plate, every man will be judged somehow or somewhat.
God put me here to let you know that nature will rise against you truly.
Every morning you pass me, you too important, you notice me not.
As if God will judge you differently, 'what do I have to do with this one?' You ask.
But God takes notes, and will judge each of you accordingly, he knows your action."

The man said, "I see the poor before the tribunal of the Almighty," the man goes on,
"With their complaints against the rich, and Christ is advocating for them,
because they refused to do what the law command." I shook my head as if I
    understood
That God created the indigents so that those who do not share can learn a lesson.
The rich are stocking everything for themselves while the poor are in debt,
But on the day of the Lord, the rich will regret the miseries they cause the needy,
Because nature will be at war with them, and who can fight the waters, the winds,
    and the fires?

I see that the rich are running for the mountains, God is mad with them for rejected
    immigrants.
The poor experience hell on earth, but God seems to say nothing, but he sees them.
I see immigrants kill themselves rather than accept incarceration, but no one cares.
Their homeland has denied them justice and freedom, those who reject them should
Wait for God, religious fanatics as you are, greedy, try to control the waters if you can.
I see both the rich and poor and dying together by tsunamis and earthquakes.

Indeed God seems to be absent everywhere, and abandons men to their shameful
Passion as they mistreat the poor, God says nothing, but judgment day is nearer
    than you think.
I see that nature and creation itself clearly identify God in their anger against
    mankind,
But many people think that everything was created by a big bang from nothing.
Humanity knows that there is a God but refuses to give him honor and glory,
And therefore, men will learn that God never relinquishes the rights to his footstool.

I see that the Judgment Day comes as a big bang, but from something, God himself.
The rich are helpless; unable to control nature, they are not able to relax as in the past.
Corruption comes to an end, and the poor are walking victoriously on a new earth.
The rich call upon God to help them, and the abusers of the indigent run fast,
But there is no place for them to hide for in their future lies death, destruction,
    and misery.
Then, I hear the indigents shout, "Rejoice! God wasn't absent in everything."

GOD'S EFFICIENT MERCY

I take refuge in the Lord. My God is an awesome God.
In his justice he saves me to go where he wants me to go.
His grace is forever sufficient, and my God is fascinating.
My God is my hope. His words I am always meditating.
How wonderful! Between the Father and us Jesus is mediating.
Such a sinner as I am, Jesus my King is always advocating.

God is never rejecting me he is my hope forever.
Jesus walks with those who follow him like bachelor.
His wondrous deeds follow even those that are irreligious.
He gives them safety and he even gives them joy as bonus.
He gives everyone rains as he gives me and heals all our pains.
His grace is so sufficient, he listen to them when they complain.

God's mercy is efficient; in his goodness he protects my brain.
I have no other ambition, but for the rest of my life to stay in his domain.
I will love my God with no condition; my mouth shall declare his mercy.
Forever Oh Lord, I will declare your justice and proclaim your beauty.
Oh Lord, my God, open my lips to proclaim your name wherever I go.
Help me take refuge in you Oh Lord, you are my God, my awesome God!

MY GOD

Here comes my God, he is my guidance
Counselor, the Almighty is here to set you free.
He's here to save you from a world of violence.
He gives me *puissance* to fly like a honeybee.
He's never absence and he gives me a heart free.

My God is the one, who says to Moses,
"I am who I am," and he is the God of Abraham.
My God is everywhere and knows all addresses.
I serve him for his boldness. He spoke to Abraham,
If I don't serve this mighty God, call me damned.

He's excellent, and he keeps me happy as I go.
"Truly the Lord is in this place," said Jacob.
The Almighty God controls the heavens above and below.
Do you know God is here? He is the one in charge of the Cherub!
He saves me from a world of violence, so to him I bow.

He will make me fly like a honeybee and to him I say bravo.
Wherever I go, my God is watching over me from a distance.
My God have mercy on me; walk with me as you did with Job.
Give me a heart free, for my God you are excellence.
My God is good. My God can set me free. He is excellence!

My mouth must proclaim his name. My God is excellence.
I was lost My God found me and he set me free.
In his omniscience, he saves me from a world of violence.
One day he will take me to heaven where I will fly like a honeybee.
My God is great! He is powerful. He gives me a heart free.

Honor and glory to my God, my God is a mighty God.
Honor and glory to my God, he breathed on the Red Sea,
He is powerful. He opened the Red Sea and told Moses to go.
My God is omnipresence. My God is not an absentee.
Implore the Lord my God. He can be yours too.

Implore my Lord, Jesus, my king. He's excellence.
Implore my Lord, Jesus, and my Savior. He can set you free.
Alleluia! He saves me from a world of violence.
In heaven, he will make me fly like a honeybee.
When I accepted my Jesus, and he gave me a heart free.

I BELIEVE

I believe God will always be on my side.
In the God of heaven I take great pride.
I have seen my God's strengths in the darkest days.
He walks with me and directs me in the right ways.

I believe in my God when my boat is sinking.
I believe in him when Satan is kicking.
I believe in my God when there seems to be no way out.
I have seen his footprint on my route.

God has a way to change my night into day.
He has a way to hear me when I pray.
God has a way to give peace to all.
He has a way to take care of our troubles, big and small.

I believe in God when the world turns upside down.
I believe in him when Satan is trying to put me down.
I believe in God to give me life after death,
And I believe my God will resurrect my soul in the new earth.

JESUS IS ALL WANT

Satan tries to make me forget my Lord,
My Jesus cut all vices in me with his sword.
Satan plants snares on my way,
Jesus saves me; that is all I have to say.

Oh, give me: Jesus is all I want.
No other seeds shall ever plant.
Jesus, Jesus, Jesus is all I want,
Jesus, Jesus, Jesus every day is all I want.

Satan stands on my left to accuse me,
By the blood of Jesus in me I redeem.
Alleluia, I redeem from danger.
Alleluia, praise the Lord; I am no longer in fear.

Oh believers, sing with me.
My Jesus is all I want.
No other seed shall ever plant.
Jesus, Jesus, Jesus is all I want,
Jesus, Jesus, Jesus every day is all I want.

SING ALONG WITH ME

Oh, Lord, my God, make me a servant, oh, my King.
I will care for the needy and walk under your covenant.
I will stay near the cross and be vigilant.
Oh, Lord, my God, in heaven for you I shall sing.

Sing, oh, vigilant, sing
to the Lord forever.
Sing, oh, militant, sing,
to the Lord forever.
Sing Alleluia, Jesus alone is king.

Listen, Oh, my friends, be wise, Oh, my brothers!
Listen, Oh, my friends, be vigilant, Oh, my sisters and others.
And be happy; God chose you to be militant.
You are to be poor in spirit, rich by faith, and vigilant.

Oh, Lord, my God, I thank you for the wisdom to love my brothers.
I thank you Lord for the wisdom to love my sisters and others.
You have chosen the needy by faith to be vigilant.
You have chosen to make us rich in heaven as militant.

MY GHOST, HOW DO YOU GET TO HEAVEN SO FAST?

You're running faster than an airplane.
You're running faster than a spacecraft.
I just went to bed and at once I am in heaven.
I am standing before the throne of God.
I see the angels dance like they have no pain.
I don't see Jesus or God this time.
An angel takes me to the temple.
I hear a big noise and something appears like flames.
I see an angel leading an admirable choir.
Oh, the choir is singing a song in beautiful rhyme.
The choir is in uniform singing with no downtime.
But how did my ghost get to heaven so fast?
The uniform has three layers of clothes.
The first and second layer is all white.
The third are blue and purple, the robe is sublime.
This is a long robe open from top to bottom.
It has a wing from the shoulder to the hip on each side.
As they raise their hands, the wings raise up with them.
Before the throne I bow, "Who is the maestro of this beautiful choir?"
Angel Gabriel said, "the maestro is the second Adam."
The basses give their back to the north as they sing.
The sopranos give their backs to the south.
The tenors stand and give their faces to the east
When I look to the west where the altos stand, I see Jesus.
I murmured, "to see something like this, I am a blessing!"
But how did my ghost get to heaven so fast?
The temple is built in the form of a football field.
There is an uncountable number of worshipers before the throne.
They take their hats and drop them before an angel that sits on the throne.
In my lifetime, I never see anything like this, the place is vast.

There are four beautiful old women standing on each corner leading the choir.,
They are singing with tears in their eyes as they drop their hats before the throne.
There are also twenty-four old men surrounding the angel who sits on the throne.
They are dropping their hats before the throne as the choir is singing.
They sing beautifully, I take my songbook and begin to sing with the choir.
Amen, amen, amen. Amen, amen, amen, Alleluia!
Forever and ever, forever and ever, Alleluia!
Jesus is King, King of kings, he is King,
Forever and ever, forever and ever, Alleluia!
Amen, Amen! Alleluia! Alleluia!
Angel Gabriel came to me and said, "I bring you here to go tell my brothers,
Jesus is alive forever and ever and he will return to judge the earth.

THE TWENTY-THIRD OF DECEMBER

I'm sitting and looking out the window.
It's better than being at war,
But I'm still thinking of a gift
For my children I hope to buy a gift,
and my heart is about to rift.

I'll put the children on my lap.
A gift does not have to wrap.
For Jesus is the true water tap.
He's the best gift
for those with a heart rift.

If I can't buy a gift,
I'll not let my heart rift.
I'll put the children on my lap
And we'll say, "Yup,
Jesus is our gift wrapped."

We won't let our hearts rift.
We'll say, "Yup,
Jesus is our gift wrapped.
And he's the best gift.
We'll not let our heart rift."

IF ANYTHING

If there's anything I'd ask for next year.
It is a chance to build God's house.
If anything I'd ask for next year,
It is for God's house to be free.
We must live in peace and without fear.
If anything I'd ask for next year
Is that we all respect God's house.
Happy New Year!

A PEOPLE WITHOUT MORALITY

When I was young, I used to hear morality speaking
We all used to hear her voice in our own mother's tongue.
"Children, the knowledge of God you should be seeking.
Children, listen to me while you are young."

And everything that used to be done was transparent.
Then society did not originate arrogance and pride.
Everyone was on morality's side, and it was apparent.
Children learned to tell the truth on their side.

Now, the foolish say, "No religion in school."
Society began to be ruled by the image of the beast.
Then they began to build more and more jails for the cruel.
Every child is acting cool; anger and crime increased.

Children die before their parent, because they are beasts.
But the foolish never learn to have sense, because they are leopard.
Nothing is done with transparency for morality fails to exist.
The fools build fences for the children [now who rule the schools and concurred.????]

Women and men are competing to reach each other.
The beasts leading the governments support the immorality.
Children take over the streets with guns. A mother calls police [for?]a father.
They began to question teachers, but how to you teach a child so bossy.

Parents can no longer discern reality. God is out of the picture.
Children walk on our streets like little beasts, they lack of morality
Society thinks morality is banality; our children are filled with anger.
A people without God are a people who cannot control their abnormality.

GO TELL

Go tell the world, the shepherd hear and see the angels sing of the messiah.
Emmanuel, Emmanuel is here to save you, Christ is here, listen to the news.
The angels of God are here to save us from obscurity. Oh children! Go call mama.
Tell mama the visitors see the star. Oh, come to see the King of the Jews.

Go tell the world this is a day to remember, this is a day of salvation.
Emmanuel is here the shepherds say; the son of God has come to stay.
This is a day for the world to remember. The diviners are here to tell the nation
He is the Christ, the King of every nation. The door of grace is opened today.

Come to see the king of the Jewish nation. Emmanuel is born in Bethlehem today.
Let's sing alleluia for the salvation. Alleluia, alleluia, for those who believe
The door of salvation is opened; this is what the shepherds are here to say.
Jesus is here to give life to all. Jesus is here to heal those who believe.

APOCALYPSE

I am a visionary. I live in a world full of misery, controlled by the power of
   darkness.

This vision of mine amazes me. I was sitting on the top floor, inside the old
   Boston Garden,

I am always predicting, and some of my hallucinations has come forth with no
   bias.

I heard a noise outside. There were no windows in the building, I sat there take
   no action.

At once a window appeared on the north side of the attic of the edifice, and I
   heard the sound

A horse galloping, and then I saw a man in the middle of the building sitting on
   the ground.

The man said, there will be three plagues falling on earth one after the other each
   as thundering.

As the one before and once you see these signs, Jesus is near to judge the world.

Then I heard noises outside, and I saw a group of men running on the streets
   each man arming.

The men's faces and hands are of goats, their feet are of humans running in our
   dream-world!"

I saw lions running after the goats; their faces are of lions, their hands and feet are
   of humans.

The lions are the poor who wear athletic shoes and are ready to fight the rich for
   their millions.

The man told me, "The goats are the rich who are about to face their judgment
   seat.

The poor of the world get together for they are angry against the rich who
   mistreat them.

The rich are richer than ever; the poor are poorer than ever. Now the rich are bear
   feet.

The man put a television before me, I saw governments everywhere falling, they
   condemn.

I saw bloods are running on our street like riverbanks and corpses filled our
   streets.

The rivers are destroyed all the resources of the earth , and there are no elite.

Then I heard God swore to the earth and heaven that he will destroy the rich
regime.
Their days are numbered, and they won't repent for they are filled with pride.
The rich make the poor work hard and don't pay them, how blaspheme!
Now the poor are taking justice in their own hands, who can control their anger!
And now the poor are asking for revenge, they will accomplish their dreams.
For God said, "The rich will never again have control over their evil regime."

Then I saw hunger is abiding on four corners of the earth and turn people to
skeletons.
Every nation is busy in its own land and none can help each other.
In the news, the government said for every man to walk around with his own
coffin.
The water is poisoned. The nations' warships are sinking, governments have no
clear answer.
I said, "Oh, God, have pity for America. Have pity for our beautiful Disneyland."
The man said I have no control over what is going on, humankind refuse to
follow God's plan.

The man said again, "America will be spared from the plague of God's anger this
time."
The news was hidden to the public, but they finally had no choice but to break it.
One quarter of the sea is poisoned. The water became bloody. It is dark in
daytime.
One quarter of the springs and one quarter of the rivers bitter, so men are falling
in their own pit.
When I heard one quarter of the sea is destroyed. I said, "Oh, God, have pity for
America."
I was amazed of what I had seen; I screamed, bow down to God the Omega and
the Alpha.

THE COMMANDMENTS LEAD ME

When you love the Lord,
You look for his award.
You worship him only.
And you'll never be lonely.

You don't promulgate his name in vain
Then you'll never suffer any pain.
You don't worship images,
This is part of God's messages.

You love others as yourself.
You follow God's laws and try to be yourself.
The Lord says, "Thou shall not kill."
Then you'll be able to see God's hill.

You don't go to bed with neither your brother's
wife neither should you go to be in your father's.
You respect your mother and father.
The Bible says, "Thou shall not steal."
Then you'll receive God's seal.

You don't make false accusations,
This is the only time you love the Lord,
And the only time you escape from malediction.
The only time you receive God's award.

A WORLD OF TUMULT

Everywhere you go men are hard-hearted.
They start wars to fill their greed.
They start chaos to fulfill their needs.
Some men are cold-hearted
But their children will repay their deeds.

Ah, men slay each other for fortune,
Ah, they need God's kind heart.
Nations will find misfortune.
They cause misdeed all over our earth,
Oh, God, give them your gentle heart.
Or they will curse the day of their birth.

I pray, Oh, Divine Creator,
Heal my broken heart.
Humans aren't apt to be negotiators.
Oh, divine, fix their weak heart.
Too much chaos in our earth
Or we will curse the day of our birth.

Master of the universe, install peace in our earth.
Give us a little of your wise heart,
Engineer of mankind,
Restore our sad heart.
So that just like you we can be kind.

PROTECT THE NEEDY

Woe to those who denied justice to others,
God won't hesitate to judge them.
They aren't my fathers and brothers.
They may be older than I am
They aren't even my friends, but it bothers
Me for they're all beloved of God, just as I am.

Never make false accusations against others,
They could have been your pop and brothers,
They could have been your mom and sisters,
This is why they can't be disregarded.
Your next of kin who is not attended.
This is one of the reasons you must love others.

The mentally retarded,
Could have been me in the same situation.
The elderly in the nursing homes are not contented
The prisoner under your care, some are in bad condition
They're human just like you; let me repeat.
We all could have been in their condition.

God asks for us to be fair.
To the woman in the operation room,
The man under arrest at your care,
God is their refuge and will deliver them soon.
I hope you don't show partiality; you should be fair.
And this is my only prayer.

GOING TO JAIL

Going to this black hole,
One should have doomed first.
One is always under control.
A sentinel is at the gate on every shift.

One can easily be raped and abused.
If one has a prior conviction,
The guards can bit you and be excused.
A friend of mine was bitten.

Depend on your means the juries are swift.
The judge refused parole and locks the prison bars.
Then you get to be abused on every shift.
You will never again be able to see the stars

Pray to God you never go to that black hole.
Politicians will brag of you to be reelected.
Believe me; you never want to be in that hellhole.
Believe me, in jail, they forced a man to eat mud.

I know one who condemned at the prison's gate.
L'état does not believe in redemption, they're inhuman.
If you end there innocently, God knows your fate.
Life in jail is hell and wherever you go it is common.

THE SCARS, I CAN'T FORGET

Have you ever been accused?
If no, you don't know what real scars are.
You would become confused.
Nobody said yet I killed someone or,
Robbed a bank, but is viable on this orb of horror.
They called me a thief.
They labeled me an abuser.
But I don't care; God is my chief.
They called me a user.
They accused me of assault.
I live under God's laws.
I pray to my God who is so good.
Satan cannot plant any of his tricks in me.
He sent Jesus in my life to do what he could.
I'll walk with God's rod till my Savior's face I'll see.

THANK YOU ONCE AGAIN

I want to thank you once again for being a true beloved.
I thank you for holding my hands and for praying with me.
I thank you for your kindness and love.
Each time I see you, I see the presence of God in my soul.
Thank you for sitting and listening to God's word with me.
Thank you for when I don't have a car you used yours as a carpool.
Thank you for the beautiful songs you sing
You encouraged me to go to heaven in your testimony.
Thank you for listening to me when I am talking.
Thank you for being my pastors and preachers,
Thank you for being the musicians that make me dance.
You show me that we are all God's creatures.
Thank you for being a friend in time of trouble.
Thank you for smiling when you see me.
You are wonderful and lovable.
Thank you for thanking me.
Thank you for being who you are,
and preach the Gospel by your love.
Again, thank you for being a beloved.
Thank you for the money you lent me and
Thank you for giving me time to pay you back
I learn from you that Christians stand
for true justice. Thank you for your comprehension.
Thank you for not backbiting me.
Thank you for the cup of coffee and the cup of tea.
Thank you for the dinner and the lunch you provided.
Thank you for going before God with my plea.
Thank you for sharing my tears and my laughter.
Thank you for not making false accusations against me.

Thank you for confessing our sins to each other.
I thank you very much.
Thank you for being a true brother.
Thank you for visiting me when I was sick.
Thank you, thank you, and thank you.
Your loving kindness is true.

BEING POOR

Being poor in this world one lacks his respect.
Is like living as a sheep without a shepherd.
Everything that happens you are a suspect.
Anything you said, you are censured.

Clans look at you like one without nobility.
Your efforts are not appreciated.
Able as you are they think you have no ability.
Discourage not you will be blessed!

Believe me brother, God clothes the skies,
As God clothes the planets and moon,
As God protects the stars and a bird that flies,
God of heaven will not let you be impugned.

As God sends the rain from above in June,
As God leads the sun to its destination at night,
God will not let you be eaten by raccoon.
Justice at last is for the poor who stay in the light.

My Friend God is for you if you stay in the light.
As long as the wind continues to blow,
So justice at last is for the poor who stay in God's sight
They will live, and the rich suffer God's woe.

THANKSGIVING DAY

We wake up early, and my brother and I began to play.
We thank Jesus who accepted to open his arms on the Cross.
We thanked God as the puritans thank God for this wonderful day.
We thank God for Jesus his son; he loves us so much he gave us the logos.

This is a day for us to share what God has given to us.
We are so happy to cook this God-given turkey.
This is a day for each one of us to learn to love, not being anxious.
We know that God always have a way to bless us, why should we be angry!

We are thankful to God for this day it doesn't matter how we eat the turkey.
Before we eat, we will pray and enjoy this wonderful day
We thank God for the Holy Spirit he poured in our hearts to make us live boldly.
Oh crown him with glory and honor, Jesus the king who gives us this day.

I HAVE FOUND THE LIVING WATER

When I met Jesus, I was in darkness, I had no delights.
I was lesser than a piece of soil on the side of the sea.
Abiding in an isolated orb where days look like nights.
I heard God's people singing, "God lifted me; God lifted me
When nothing else could help, God lifted me," then I saw
By faith my Savior Jesus on the cross dying for me.

Oh! I have found a fountain of living water.
I filled my cup; I drank until I was satisfied.
I have found peace at the cross for that matter.
Oh! What a joy knowing, with Jesus I am justified.

Oh! Come today at the feet of the cross where there's room.
Where there is a spring of living water.
Oh! Aren't you afraid like me of the cold and want to find a room?
Come to drink the living water, and it doesn't matter
How sinful you are; at the cross there is room.
All mankind can gather under his protection, sinner, it doesn't mater.

Jesus the light of the world will give you delights.
And some day he will take you beyond the sea.
To his kingdom where there will be no nights
And some day in heaven, Jesus's face you'll see.

ON THE MOUNTAIN OF GOD

On the mountain of God, Jesus went to build a mansion for me.
On the mountain of God, it's where my final destination will be.
On the mountain of God, Jesus saves a surprise for me.
On the mountain of God, Jesus' handsome face I will see.

On the mountain of God, that's where my sorrow will end.
On the mountain of God, I will have no more tears in that land.
On the mountain of God, the prophets' faces I will see.
On the mountain of God, it's where my final destination will be.

On the mountain of God, the angels' faces I will see,
On the mountain of God, I will sing Alleluia.
On the mountain of God, I will walk in my mansion.
On the mountain of God, I will sing glory to God, Alleluia!

On the mountain of God, before the throne of God I will stand,
To listen to the living creatures and the elders sing a new song.
On the mountain of God, I will have no more tears in that land.
On the mountain of God, that's where my soul will be where there is no end.

IS GOD PART OF THE SCHEME?

If I were a music writer, I would write a verse.
I would write about how the rich control the universe.
They are creating corporations to control the poor with their might.
But I swear before God Almighty, the rich are not bright.

Just as the air can penetrate wherever it wishes to be,
So the rich are in control of everything on earth and the sky.
The poor are living on earth miserably, including me.
But surely, God is watching us; the poor even with one eye.

The banks are putting high interest rates on us on their part.
Our governments overtax us on everything to force us to die.
A rich man I know is evil and do not seem to have a heart.
If there is a God, he must be watching his actions with an eye.

Look at the gas prices everywhere; how can I buy a liter of it, poor me?
Look at my car insurance; it's so high; how can I pay it, poor me?
If God is not part of the scheme, I am waiting patiently to see his might.
It's gotten so bad; I hope God will have a talk with the rich tonight.

Go to the supermarket, look at food prices; tell me if I can buy it, poor me.
Look at the price of heath insurance; tell me if I can afford it, poor me.
Look at the governmental jobs, check to see if you see people like me.
Believe me; the poor are living on earth miserably, including me.

I BELIEVE SOME DAY

I believe some day the earth will change into a heaven.
Humans will fly, fly, fly like the birds into the moon.
The animals will talk like the humans, and they will say, "It is eleven."
I believe we will live on earth just like the angels in heaven soon.

I believe some day the earth will change into a heaven.
Humans will be fully reasonable, and there will be no wars.
The weak will sit at the same table as the strong in heaven.
I believe some day humans will no longer sleep in closed doors.

I believe some day snakes will come to witness a new birth.
There will be no jails to lock each other up no more.
I believe some day there will be no more hatred on earth.
I believe some day humans will no longer sleep in closed doors.

I believe some day humans and angels will marry each other.
I believe some day animals will say to humans, "Give me your gun."
I believe some day countries will be run by civilians, and people will care for each other.
I believe some day we will have no need for an army, Oh, that will be fun.

I believe some day nature will be peaceful on the four corners of the earth.
I believe some day humans or animals will have no fear of the waters and sea.
I believe some day the earth will be peaceful and will be as sweet as a new birth.
I believe some day the animals and reptiles will sit next to me.

THE CHURCH

I dreamed I went to a city in heaven, what a dream!
I went to your wedding where there was a magnificent stream.
Yeah! You lay in your mansion, resting with your sweetheart.
I looked at the beauty of your home, what splendid art!

Your dress was so splendid my eyes could not pervade through it.
Your fine dress made by the hand of God, and it was perfectly fit.
You married with the Lamb, the one that pledged to marry you.
Oh! I saw him abide on earth! God's promises are just and true.

He moved with you to the awe-inspiring habitation he built with precious stone.
He dwells with you in the Holy City of God where there won't be any cyclone.
Oh I saw the lamb as King on the new earth! God's promises are true and just.
Feel at ease, you are now married with the Lamb whom you trust.

Your home is ascending in Jerusalem, where visitors can come for a tour.
Oh, how sweet! How marvelous it is for the Lamb of God to be your sweetheart!
You are now abiding in a haven shining with the glory of you God , lets praise Him
    therefore.
and I looked at the beauty of your home, what splendid art?

You accepted to suffer, lived on earth as poor,
But now look at you in a home built with jasper, brilliant for sure.
You accepted to be persecuted because of him who died for you.
But now look at how the leaders of the world are carrying their wealth to you.

Now, you have the security you have been longing for.
You sleep in your attractive dwelling with an open door.
Visitors can come from all over the world to visit you.
And nothing impure can enter your mansion for evermore. Amen! Alleluia!

FOR THE THOUSAND YEARS OF JESUS' REIGN

For a thousand years, I am voting for Jesus my Lord.
He reigns forever and ever, forever and ever.
For a thousand years, there will be no coup d'état as my reward.
For a thousand years, there will be no false elections and then forever.
For a thousand years, Jesus will alone reign as King and Lord.

For a thousand years, I hear no lie.
For a thousand years, I live without pain.
For a thousand years, humans no longer die.
For a thousand years, Satan is tied in chains.
For a thousand years, I hear no wars.
For a thousand years, I hear no news of terrors and live in open doors.

For a thousand years, Jesus reigns as a conqueror.
For a thousand years, I have no tears in my eyes.
For a thousand years, I have not heard from even a creditor.
For a thousand years, I never cry.
For a thousand years, peace abide on earth,
And after one thousand years, Jesus proves that he is wise.
For a thousand years, Jesus took power from death.
Alleluia!
Amen!

MY SWEET JESUS

It is good and sweet to talk to you at noon.
It is awesome to convey with you in prayer in the afternoon.
My sweet Jesus, I know that you are coming soon.
Oh! I can't wait to travel with you soon!

It is good and sweet to meet with Jesus at noon.
Jesus is good and sweet not only in the new moon.
Oh! With Jesus it is always a honeymoon.
Ah! My heart can't wait to see his beautiful face soon.

Oh! It is sweet to live by his grace and mercy at noon.
Oh! It is sweet and beautiful to wait for the honeymoon
Oh! I can't wait to see his precious face soon.
Oh! Jesus is sweet in the morning and at noon.
Amen!
Alleluia!

WHEN I FELL IN LOVE WITH CHRIST

I was young and living without hope.
I found the Gospel; I tied it around me like a rope.
Jesus came to my life and satisfied my hunger.
And he gave me the Holy Spirit as a souvenir.

My sweet Jesus, I surrender to your constant love.
My sweet Jesus, you are my King living above.
My sweet Jesus, in you I find protection.
My sweet Jesus, I give you all my adoration.

My sweet Jesus, under your care I live one day at a time.
My sweet Jesus, it is good to sing your name with flawless rhyme.
My sweet Jesus, I surrender to your constant love.
My sweet Jesus, you are my king living above.

Amen!
Alleluia!

THE RIDER ON THE WHITE HORSE

He is Jesus the King of kings and Lord of salvation.
He is the one being called, "faithful and true."
He is the warrior that can fight with precision and is the true incarnation.
He is the warrior to win the battle for you.

Jesus is already victorious in the fight.
He is the general that's in control of God's army.
He is a warrior with a strong might.
Jesus has already won the battle over his enemy.

When Jesus reigns, corrupt leaders of the earth will give in their resignations.
The rider on the white horse is the only one that can give salvation.
No warrior can ever fight my Lord.
He is the only one who will give a true reward.

Amen!
Alleluia!

WHEN I WAS YOUNG

When I was young, I wanted God only.
I never wanted to be among the sinners.
I wanted to serve God with all my heart fully.
I served Jesus in everything as my savior.
Ah, I met a woman who had no respect for the son of man.
She was filled with the spirit of Jezebel.
Lacked of the spirit of discernment, my troubles began.
Still, I trusted God, with my soul it is all well.

Alas! A young man should listen to God's command.
One says, "If God was so good, how can you divorce now?"
Well, I met with temptation, my soul could not withstand
Well, I let a woman share God's glory somehow.
Then I become worthless in the eyes of God.
Come closer to hear what God had to say:
"I am the first, the last, the only God."
O! A young man should know Jesus is the only way.

O, with my soul it is well I listened to wisdom.
I put my trust in God, no sinful men could entice me.
I prayed to God all mighty not to become my enemy's victim.
I saw young men despised wisdom who hurt badly.
I went to God and confessed since I knew he held success
In his store for those who are wise and trusted him.
The more I walked with him the more I made progress.
I stayed with him til in his amazing grace I swim.

AT THE AGE OF FIVE

At the age of five, I met Pastor Gabriel.
He said to me, "God has done great things for Israel.
God can do many things for you too if you live as a sentinel."
He taught me how spiritually I could excel.

God can do great things for those who follow his commands.
God told me many things as I followed his demands.
I prayed and gave thanks to the Lord day and night.
God sent his angels to speak to me every night.

Oh! I served the Lord who gave Eli power over the rain.
Now I am forty-eight, and I hear God talking to me again.
He tells me to tell the world Jesus will be coming with a reward.
He will bless Every man who loves him and calls him Lord.

HOW CAN I FORGET?

I will never forget I was very sick, and I went for a checkup.
The cyst made me unable to raise my chin up.
The doctor told me that I was not going to live; I cried to the Lord,
I begged him to save my life; he healed me as a reward.

Doctors say that death was imminent, and I was upset.
I did not lose hope though the cyst stood next to me like a coquette.
My family lost hope and told me the cyst was the work of the diabolic.
Alleluia! I was not afraid, but the cyst made me melancholic.

Nobody thought I was going to live. I went to bed I could not get up.
Everywhere I went with my disease I was mocked at.
With the Holy Spirit in me I was able to control my emotions.
My faith told me, "You heal. God is the master of earth and the ocean."

I spent five years with the cyst, and I could not raise my head up.
I spent twelve months in the hospital, seeking treatment.
The Lord healed me in matter of seconds. Oh, how excellent!
Help me praise the Lord Almighty who has raised me up!

CLOSE UP

When you are with someone you really love.
You always want to be closer and closer to the friend,
So when you love the Lord who lives above,
You want to be closer and closer to him till the end.

It is better to abandon an old friend than God.
That's the only time he speaks to you like a beloved.
He will be with you even when you travel abroad.
The closer you are with God the more you know his love.

The closer you are with God the more you remain modest.
Your respect for him prove by your action and words.
A man who stay close to God will be called the humblest.
One stays close with God he gives him the strength of leopards.

COMING, MY SWEET JESUS

I heard Jesus speak into my ear.
"Everyone, who thirsts, come; what are you waiting for."
Jesus said again into my ear.
"I am standing at your door,
If you hear my voice, I will come to eat super with you."

Coming, my sweet Jesus; eat super with me.
Coming, my sweet Jesus; I'd love to eat with you.
Coming, my sweet Jesus comes to sit beside me.
Coming, my sweet Jesus give me a new name too.

I heard Jesus speak into my ear,
He said, "Turn away from sin; come to me."
Once more he speaks into my ear,
He said to me, "I love thee."
Then I came to Jesus; he took my fears away.

Oh, glory for me!

YES, LORD!

When I understood the Gospel,
My heart turns into a garden,
The word filled me in the chapel.
It was as sweet as a fruit from the Garden of Eden.

Oh, I heard the voice of Jesus said,
"I am your Lord and Savior; I will make you a Nazarene.
I am your engineer and doctor to refine and heal you every day.
Come to me with your burden,
And I will give you rest, and in your troubles I will intervene."

God had chosen me to be a Nazarene.
He has elected me to serve him as the creator of all things.
Oh, I shouted for joy, when I heard the voice from heaven
It was the voice of God who created everything.

Oh yeah! The Gospel is God's power.
It saves me from the ruin of sin.
Oh, I thank God through Jesus Christ my engineer.
He gives me the Gospel to improve my life like a vitamin.

ON THE DAY OF PENTECOST

The Holy Spirit descended from heaven to earth like rain,
As Jesus sent the comforter to fulfill what was preordained.
Peter preached, and everyone heard what the Holy Spirit had to say.
Those who believed were filled with the Holy Ghost on that day.

On the Day of Pentecost, Christians empower with God's love.
Let us pray to God so that we too will do wonders in the name of God above.
I pray for every day of my life to be like the Day of Pentecost
Forever I want to proclaim God's message to those that are lost.

Like the Day of Pentecost, I too escape from malediction.
Oh, Holy Ghost, teach us to stay together to find benediction.
If we allow God to fill us with the Holy Ghost, we will do wonders,
And like Peter, I want to become a pioneer for my Lord.

On the Day of Pentecost, the Holy Spirit fell down to men.
On the Day of Pentecost, the believers filled with power.
Everyone saw wonders coming down like shower,
To the sweet word of the Gospel, all that listened said, "Amen!"

Amen!
Alleluia!
Amen!
Alleluia!

I STAND IN AWE

I stand in awe,
I see the night, trimmed in black, nearing to intersect with the day.
I stand in awe,
The morning comes as a beauty queen, and I say, "Ah!"
He announced to all humanity to follow God's law.

I stand in awe,
I see the sky gushing above my head declare the glory of God.
I stand in awe,
I see the sun nearing out of his home with his splendid eyes, I say "Ah!"

I stand in awe,
I see the birds that God created are flying in the air,
They proclaim the glory of God with their wings.
I said, oh! God is worthy to be praised, ah!

I stand in awe,
When I see sinners like me singing for God.
I stand in awe,
When I know that God build a home in heaven
Oh! God is worthy to be praised, ah!

ONE MORE OBSERVATION

I observed these things:
Only stupid people abuse others.
Only stupid people hurt others.
Only stupid people hate others.
Only stupid people seek revenge.
Intelligent people don't hurt their brothers.
Stupid people always look strange.
Stupid people are those lacking the love of God.
Stupid people never repent.
Stupid people say there is not a God.
They only seek God when they are in trouble.
How can they find God when they need him?

JESUS WILL BE THERE

There is a friend that will always be there.
When there is war everywhere and nobody wants peace.
When there is famine and earthquake everywhere.
Jesus will be there to set peace.

When the moon will no longer shine
There is a friend that will always be there.
When the brightness of the sun will decline,
Trust in Jesus; he will be there.

There is a friend that will always be there.
When your pride, comrade, pushes you away,
When your best friend seems not to care,
Trust in Jesus, he will be there.

Trust in Jesus when the moon no longer shines.
Have faith in the Savior when the sun turns dark.
Hold firmly to your hope when you see no good signs.
Jesus will be there just like God was there in Noah's ark.

THE WORLD NEEDS ONE THING

The world needs the Lord.
Every time I turn on the television,
I realize the world needs the Lord.
I can only see and hear division.

There will be no discussion on *Roe v. Wade*.
There will be security in our hemisphere.
There won't be a need for military recruiter,
If the world decides to accept the Lord.

The world needs the Lord as a friend.
The discussion of white versus black will end.
The discussion of terrorists will end.
The discussion of war will end.
The discussion of hunger will end.

I listened to politicians in the west.
I listened to those from the east.
I listened to those from the south.
I listened to them from the north.
They lack one thing: the Lord as their priest.

A MAN NAMED STEPHEN

There was a man by the name of Stephen, God's appointee.
He took courage to talk about Jesus, the man of Galilee.
He told the Israelites their sinful hearts are by God forbidden
He asked them to stop resisting the Holy Spirit as their fathers did.

Instead of repenting, they killed the man sent by God.
They gnashed at Stephen with their teeth and that was fraud.
They resisted God and killed a man God sent into the world.
Ah, without pity, they stoned Stephen and take back their dream world.

Fear not, my dear sisters; fear not, my dear brothers.
Fear not, my dear God's people, to this earth you are strangers.
As Stephen, you may be persecuted for Jesus too,
But Jesus is standing at the right hand of God to receive you.

Today, there are many that resist the Holy Spirit.
They are preachers but stiff-necks and hypocrites.
Some of your persecutors are pastors and church members too.
Fear not for you serve the Alpha and the Omega who will deliver you.

DANIEL DANCED IN THE LIONS' DEN

Long time ago there was a young man by the name of Daniel.
He was taken into the captivity in Babylon to dwell.
Daniel obeyed God and refused to defile himself as God's sentinel.
He set himself as God's servant in the King's citadel.

God always stands with those that obey him.
God always walk with those that trust in him,
As did Daniel, Shadrach, Meshach, and Abed-Nego,
Ask God to walk with you as you go.

The Chaldeans accused the Jews of refusing to obey the King,
As a servant of Jesus in this world you can be accused for your faith,
But remember young Daniel in the lions' den; he tried to sing,
The God he serves delivered him from the mouth of the lions by faith.

The king gave the command for Daniel to be thrown in the lions' den.
As Daniel arrived in the den he began to praise
God and God sent his angels to shut the lions' mouth in the den.
The God of Daniel is capable to deliver you from the maze.

The King woke up and believed that the lions had eaten Daniel.
The King sadly called Daniel in the lions' den
The King knew that Daniel was God's sentinel.
The King commanded his guards to take Daniel out of the lions' den.
Daniel had no injury; the angels of God danced with him in the den.

A MAN NAMED JOB

In the land of Uz, there was a man named Job.
Job trusted God and in the eyes of God he was honest.
He knew that God has control of this globe.
He turned against evil as a realist.

Satan went before the Lord and accused Job.
But after Satan attacked Job, Job became more faithful.
God trusted Job; Job also wore faith in God as a robe.
Satan struck Job in everything, but he stayed under God's rule.

Oh, God! Help me to be as faithful as Job!
Job was rich, and he lost everything.
Job knew that everything is vanity in this globe.
He lost his children, but God returned everything.

Job put nothing between him and God on this globe.
He owned three thousand camels, seven thousand sheep.
As the Lord had said, there had never been a man as faithful as Job.
He trusted God even when the news made him weep.

Sometimes Satan makes us weep.
Job wept too after he lost one thousand cattle.
He owned five hundred donkeys and seven thousand sheep.
He also had many servants, but to his God all these were little.

What can you compare to your God?
Job's friend gave up on him,
But Job knew that God could carry his load.
Job stood with God even when his wife gave up on him.

Job said, "I was born with nothing.
I will die with nothing."
Job praised God's name in everything.
If we believe like Job, God will bless us in everything.

Look at Job; he was a man of faith.
The world gave up on him, but God was there.
It is like that today, if we keep our faith,
God will make a difference in our lives as the great engineer.

HADES

You've warned me not to go there
O! Preacher! But I'm not sure,
What you're saying, preacher!
You say hell is fiery atmosphere.
You say not place for impure.
But you are impure and insincere.

You say hell is a place of misery.
It is infernal regions and a bottomless pit.
It is Satan's kingdom, a lake of fire
But you know that you are a mercenary.
How many of God's children you smite?
Yeah! You steal church money, liar!

You said, "It's a place of madness.
It's a place of torment,
It is a place for anguish, agony, wretchedness."
You say hell is preeminent.
This earth is the house of Jezebel?
You believe in wars, and mistreatment to the poor
Don't you contribute to make the earth feel like hell?

THE FIGHT WITH BEING

Oh! I do not feel like I am existing.
I am living in affliction and pain.
Sometimes I do not want to be bugging.
And some day I feel like I am in chains.
Oh God knows, everything I tried, I fail.
But I will always be energetic and lively.
Although it feels like my life want to derail.
My frustration every day is in a greater scale.
I do my best to say to "Failure, adieu
When I can't hold down and losing my virtue.
I know there is such a thing as being.
God is a being and there is also failure
Failure is also a being that is cursing.
Life in failure is deadlier than a cancer.
Success is also being that changes one life
Is the reason I do my best to say to failure adieu!
It is better to live in poverty than being rich in strife.
I want to hold down and never to lose my virtue.
When I am with failure I become a debtor.
I pray to the almighty to deliver me from failure.
Oh! Captain of ocean, earth, and sky
Life is difficult, it put me into silence.
She locks the port of success thereby
She causes success in my life to be absent.
Oh, God of heaven! Help me be hopeful.
Help me be strong and keep my head high.
Take failure away in my life I will be thankful.
Failure! You can't set me down, you have no *vie*.
Thank God failure ran away, I am hopeful.
I will not invite her in my life, I'll be watchful.

IT'S MIDNIGHT

It's midnight.
It's time to ring the church's bell.
It's midnight; let's sing together tonight.
Ah! Ah! Jesus Christ is here to dwell.

It's midnight; let's proclaim Jesus tonight.
Ah! Ah! Jesus comes to earth to dwell.
Ah! Ah! Let the children laugh tonight.
Ah! Ah! In Bethlehem everything is well.

It's midnight, and a silent night.
Oh in Bethlehem it is well in every heart.
Ah! Ah! Jesus is here, all is right.
Open your mind and let Jesus dwell in your heart.

Jesus is here! Let's be happy under the sun.
Jesus Christ is born today.
Ah! Ah! Come to see the Son of Man.
Jesus Christ is here to stay.